The *Burden* of **Prophetic Ministry**

Dr. Delisa Rodgers

The Burden of Prophetic Ministry

The Holy Bible, Berean Study Bible, BSB
Copyright ©2016 by Bible Hub
Used by Permission. All Rights Reserved Worldwide.

Unless otherwise stated, all Scripture quotations are taken from the
King James Version of the Holy Bible. All Rights Reserved.

New American Standard Bible Copyright © 1960 - 1995 by The
Lockman Foundation.

Published by Liberty River Industries
5201 Ste D Nations Ford Road
Charlotte, NC 28217
980-292-1754

Edited by Delisa Rodgers
Cover design: Delisa Rodgers

LIBERTY RIVER
INDUSTRIES, LLC

DEDICATION

This book is dedicated to every prophet or prophetic believer who has felt like they were going crazy. It is to encourage you through those times when you know you hear God, yet no one seems to understand you. And it serves to reason that, yes, prophets are different, and though the world may not understand it and the church may resist it, we are still comfortable with who we are and Whose we are.

TABLE OF CONTENTS

Give instruction to a wise man, and he will be yet wiser:

teach a just man, and he will increase in learning. –

PROVERBS 9:9

-1-
The Burden of The Lord in Prophetic Ministry

Zechariah 12:1, "The burden of the word of the LORD concerning Israel. Thus declares the LORD who stretches out the heavens, lays the foundation of the earth, and forms the spirit of man within him."

In a time when apostles and prophets are being more realized than ever, a thorough understanding of the purpose and intention of prophetic ministry is paramount to every believer, whether they are called a prophet or not. With the rise and popularity of prophetic circles, it is expedient that every believer equips themselves with knowledge for how to discern what is false or immature amongst the prophetic. While it is true that a prophet can be immature yet easily misplaced as false due to ignorance, one must be able to discern the difference between a prophetic word that is underdeveloped and one that has its origin in the satanic.

Although a rich outlet for sharing and enlightening among the believers, social media also serves as a sinister tool of satan to deceive many into exalting themselves into a prophetic office. Understand that all Spirit-filled believers are equipped with prophetic giftings. Still, only those elected by God through the agency of the Holy Spirit are appointed to function in the prophetic office. Specific social media users have combined the two and caused many to frustrate their callings by claiming an office for which they are not graced. There have been church splits, fights, discord, and division over 'prophetic words' released over social media that more senior and mature elder prophets have never judged. Additionally, prophetic conferences, teleconferences, schools of prophets, and such have been created and fostered off the backs of trending social media users' posts where too many men and women of God are being bamboozled into gimmicks, carnality, and spectacles, all in the name of prophetic ministry. There is no wonder such confusion, distrust, and lack of integrity among prophetic ministries. The enemy has infiltrated it, undermined it, and caused many to despise it.

God sends His minister-prophets mainly to social media to uproot, tear down, pluck up, and replant. Granted, some men and women of God are genuinely called to the mountain of media for these very purposes. Despite what the enemy has planned for social media, God sends His prophets to Facebook, Twitter, Google+, TV,

Radio, YouTube, etc., to reach and teach nations about Him. These prophets and prophetic peoples will carry the burden of the Lord, the heart of the Lord, and most importantly, the word of the Lord to a lost and misdirected generation. They will communicate the present mind of the Lord to His people so that they can intelligently and truthfully serve and worship Him.

Why is there a burden in prophetic ministry?

A burden is defined as a heavy weight or load. It is something cumbersome to bear. According to the Free Dictionary, "a burden is something that is carried or that which has great emotional difficulty."

Although Jesus told us to cast our cares upon Him, the Lord God casts His burdens for mankind upon the prophets. For an Almighty Creator God to expect a frail human being to carry His burden is significant; thus, to bear the burden of the Lord is to be concerned with what touches His heart. It is to discern how He is feeling about a matter. And it is to hear His voice and convey it as closely as possible to what you've been told without adding your rhetoric, tone, and feelings. It is a thing to die for.

When you understand that prophets and prophetic people carry God's burdens, you must know that they are mature enough to handle the wide range of emotions the Lord can express without allowing their personal feelings to become involved. When God gives someone His burdens, He is sharing His secrets. He does not share them with just anyone. Those with whom He chooses to share His burdens are highly trustworthy, seasoned, proven, and stable individuals. Consider this in your personal life. Would you share your burdens with a total stranger? Would you write them on the walls at your place of employment? Would you share them with the first people you meet at the coffee shop, or would you hold them within until you've deemed a person worthy of handling your business? The latter rings true, of course.

-2-
God's Word And
His Burden

Malachi 1:1, "The burden of the word of the lord."

When God has a burden, He has a BURDEN! When He draws near the mind or ear gate of the prophetic person with a burden, He has serious concerns to share. When God dispatched Joshua's spies to Jericho, He expressed a burden for Rahab and her family. In His infinite mind, He knew she would receive salvation by faith for her household, so before

He could allow the destruction of Jericho, He impressed upon Joshua to send spies to her city. Then He intentionally directed the spies to Rahab's place of establishment.

Joshua 2:1, "And Joshua the son of Nun sent out of Shittim two men to spy secretly, saying, Go view the land, even Jericho. And they went into a harlot's house, named Rahab, and lodged there."

When God appeared to Abraham to discuss His intentions of destroying Sodom and Gomorrah, He had burdens for Abrahams and his family. He knew by a divine selection that Lot would be spared, but He laid His burden on Abraham that he might intercede on Lot's behalf.

Genesis 18:22, "And the men turned their faces from thence, and went toward Sodom: but Abraham stood yet before the Lord."

Again, when God appeared to Abraham to announce Sarah's conception, although the child, Isaac, was a gift from God, it was also His burden to birth the chosen race of people.

The Lord does not share His burdens with simpletons who can't fathom how He feels and would care less even if they did. People's lives are at stake. When Sarah laughed at God's burden to plant Isaac in the earth, He interrogated and embarrassed her. The Lord expects us to take His burdens seriously. He immediately confronted Sarah; therefore, what God has in mind for this present age and the age to come is no laughing matter. He deals abundantly with those who are sober, vigilant, and mature.

In the Law of Moses, the Lord intended for the priests to carry the burden (or the total weight) of the ark of the covenant of the Lord on their shoulders. They were to *feel* the *heaviness* of what they carried. They were to *become one* with the burden of the Lord and own that responsibility. Years later, when David attempted to transport the ark to Jerusalem, he fashioned a 'new' ox cart. Why he thought a 'new' ox cart would impress the Lord to betray His word is beyond me, but many 'kings' have followed that same pursuit in this very hour. They have fashioned something new, but God did not ordain anything new to usher in His glory. He expects His word to be followed to the letter and complied with, and then we shall see His glory displayed in full splendor.

Uzzah died because David dishonored the Lord by disrespecting the law of Moses as it pertained to the priests carrying the burden of the ark. The same applies today. When a prophet or any minister answers the call to carry the word of the Lord, the Lord gives them His burden because He expects them to feel His hurt, disappointment, anger, and remorse over a matter. Consider the following emotional expressions given by God to His prophets.

*Genesis 6:6-7, "And it **repented** the*

LORD that he had made man on the earth, and it grieved him at his heart. And the LORD said, I will destroy man whom I have created from the face of the earth; both man, and beast, and the creeping thing, and the fowls of the air; for it repenteth me that I have made them."

1 Samuel 15:11, "It **repenteth** me that I have set up Saul to be king: for he is turned back from following me, and hath not performed my commandments. And it grieved Samuel; and he cried unto the LORD all night."

Isaiah 63:10, "But they rebelled, and **vexed** his holy Spirit: therefore he was turned to be their enemy, and he fought against them."

Exodus 32:11, "And Moses besought the LORD his God, and said, LORD, why doth thy **wrath** wax hot against thy people, which thou hast brought forth out of the land of Egypt with great power, and with a mighty hand."

Amos 7:6, "The LORD **repented** for this: This also shall not be, saith the Lord GOD."

When words such as these are delivered to His prophets and ministers, that person picks up His burden. They sense His anguish, His frustration, and His fierceness. God's emotions can be a dreadful thing to experience. Mind, for most of these prophets' lives, they lived alone. Most people hated to see them come, mainly if they lived in sin and rebellion. When a prophet was sent to a tribe or a town in the Old Testament, it was not to give the word such as what we experience in our conferences today. When God sent His prophets in times past, it was to correct them, deliver judgment, perform an ordination, declare war, or reconcile the people to their God. Even now, this is still the main thrust of authentic prophetic ministry. The prophets are sent according *to Jeremiah 1:10, "See, I have this day set thee over the nations and the kingdoms, **to root out, and to pull down, and to destroy, and to throw down, to build, and to plant."***

To carry the burden of the Lord is a weighty assignment that is not shared with the double-minded, unstable, or cowardly. God has to trust those He sends with His burdens to not defect on the day of battle or in the face of adversity. He has tested His own to see if they can stand under His burden's pressure. Just as the Lord sifted Gideon's army, the Lord has also sifted His own. He knows who will stand in the evil day. He knows who will overcome. He knows who will resist the enemy and cause him to flee. And He also knows who will buckle, bend, and undeniably bow to the works of Satan.

Isaiah 50:7, "For the Lord GOD will help me; therefore shall I not be confounded: therefore have I set my face like a flint, and I know that I shall not be ashamed."

Ezekiel 3:9, "As an adamant harder than flint has I made thy forehead: fear them not, neither be dismayed at their looks, though they be a rebellious house."

Those carrying the Lord's burden must set themselves as His burden carriers. Though the load gets heavy to bear, it is also their delight. They take pleasure in partnering with the Lord. Just as a friend loves to draw close to another friend in times of anxiety and despair, so must God's burden bearers draw close to feel out His heart and convey it to those who concern Him. They must become one with the burden. In other words, they internalize the burden. They take it personally. The power in delivering the burden of the Lord is proven by its experience and the passion in which it is shared.

-3-
Becoming One With
The Lord's Burden

Ezekiel 3:1-4, "Moreover he said unto me, Son of man, eat that thou findest; eat this roll, and go speak unto the house of Israel. So I opened my mouth, and he caused me to eat that roll. And he said unto me, Son of man, cause thy belly to eat, and fill thy bowels with this roll that I give thee. Then did I eat it; and it was in my mouth as honey for sweetness. And he said unto me, Son of man, go, get thee unto the house of Israel, and speak with my words unto them."

Prophecy is artesian. In other words, it is the product of that which has been released in a man's belly. When God gives you a word, the sole experience of being in His presence to receive such a profound message is a life-changing one. However, grief sets in when the word settles in your belly, and your spirit man prepares to digest what the Lord has said. Many receive the word with great joy, but delivering such a word can be very difficult. The more the Lord reveals to you, the heavier the burden becomes to bear because you are now seeing as He sees, and you hear as He hears, and to carry such profound knowledge, is an incredible experience.

What are the burdens of the Lord?

John 3:16, "For God so loved the world, that he gave his only begotten Son, that whosoever believeth in him should not perish, but have everlasting life."

God's burden is *always* the salvation of mankind. Nothing means more to Him than restoring man's relationship with Him. God loves family, and He loves to care for the family. To see the family prosper in every aspect is always on His mind.

Romans 11:29, "For the gifts and calling of God are without repentance."

God has gifted each of us. As such,v He fully expects His gifts to be used to expand His Kingdom and bring Him glory. Therefore, knowing someone is abusing or misusing these gifts is a burden.

Matthew 19:6, "Wherefore they are no more twain, but one flesh. What therefore God hath joined together, let not man put asunder."

To see marriages fail is a burden on the Lord. He loves and cherishes the institution of marriage, and it is His will that every marriage He joined remains strong and lasts until death.

Matthew 16:18, "And I say also unto thee, That thou art Peter, and upon this rock I will build my church; and the gates of hell shall not prevail against it."

The church is a burden of the Lord. He expects His churches to be houses of prayer, a refuge, and a place of strength for the weary. He expects sons and daughters from the Church to teach nations about Him. He has a burden for the Church to make disciples of the Lord Jesus Christ.

To recap, the significant burdens of the Lord are personal salvation, the family, stewardship of spiritual gifts, marriages, and the Church. Every mountain of culture is affected by these five significant burdens. Every aspect of the marketplace is affected by these five, and hell also responds to them. So as a prophetic believer, in which areas do you think the Lord would expect His prophets to speak and teach? One of these five, undoubtedly.

Now some may say, "Where is money? Why isn't that important?" Money will come. Money is the fruit of work and effort, but God doesn't want us to love money. Money is our servant. It responds when we work for it, demand it, and are worthy of it. It is not a burden of the Lord, nor should it be ours. We need money to live, but we don't live by money. Our minds must be centered around pleasing God and using the gifts He has given us; then, the money will come.

*Matthew 6:33, "But seek ye **first** the kingdom of God, and his righteousness; and **all these things shall be added unto you**."*

This page left intentionally blank.

-4-

The Burden Of
Old Testament Prophets

The Bible records seventeen books written by the prophets. If we were to include the Pentateuch, the first five books of Moses, the total would be twenty-one. And if we were to include Samuel's two books, the Psalms of David and the Proverbs of King Solomon, we would arrive at twenty-five prophetic books! Out of thirty-nine Old Testament books, twenty-five were written by prophets or about prophets. What does that tell you about the burden of the Lord to His prophets? There were many.

Let us look at each of the seventeen prophetic books to surmise the burden of the Lord on the prophets.

The burden of the Lord to Prophet Isaiah was to warn the people of the judgment to come against sinful Judah. He also foretold the Messiah's birth to a virgin and prophesied the new Heaven and new earth. He is known as the 'evangelical prophet' because he was only the preacher of the gospel of Jesus Christ in the Old Testament. He preached against ungodliness and idolatry and summoned the nation of Israel to repentance. He was hated by King Ahaz and loved by King Hezekiah even though Hezekiah didn't always heed his advice.

The burden of the Lord to Prophet Jeremiah was an emotional one. He had to preach more judgment to an already fallen Judah and compel the people to surrender to Nebuchadnezzar. He preached against apostasy and was most often in spiritual anguish. He served as the Lord's watchman, warrior, and witness of Judas' trespasses against the Lord.

The burden of the Lord to Prophet Jeremiah in Lamentations was to weep and intercede for Jerusalem as Babylon invaded them. What he prophesied was unfolded in Lamentations. Nevertheless, the prophet took up lamenting and weeping for his people instead of an' I told you so' attitude. Jeremiah is a watchman, but in Lamentations, he is an intercessor over the disasters of Judah as they are given to Nebuchadnezzar as slaves to Babylon. A prophet's burden assignment can change from one extreme to another.

The burden of the Lord to Prophet Ezekiel was to prophesy Jerusalem's fall and then her restoration. He suffered the death of his wife as he executed the Lord's assignments. His assignment was stern, harsh, and almost heartless. He carried the word of the Lord to the captives of Babylon and those who remained at home. Ezekiel was a man of vision and a seer who gave us an illusion of the Kingdom of God.

The burden of the Lord to Prophet Daniel was to comfort the faithful during the time of Babylonian captivity under Nebuchadnezzar. To Daniel, it was given the apostasy or falling away of God's people, the revelation of man, the tribulation, the second coming of Christ, the millennial reign, and the Day of Judgment. The burden of the Lord on Daniel is just as significant to our day and time as it was for his.

The burden of the Lord to Prophet Hosea was to preach against the unfaithfulness of Israel, her punishment, and ultimate restoration. He was assigned to preach conviction of sin and bring the people to repentance. He deals with the ignorance of the people that leads to their destruction, and he consistently calls them back home with God.

The Lord allows Hosea to emotionally and physically experience His burden by allowing his wife, Gomer, to play the harlot.

The burden of the Lord to Prophet Joel was to expound on the locust plague and how they signified future judgment. He prophesied to them that they would return to a future place in God beyond their judgment. He prophesied that they would be Spirit-filled and prophesied the rise of prophetic people- you and me.

The burden of the Lord to Prophet Amos was to call the people back to God. He preached reconciliation with the Lord. He deals with hidden religiosity and spiritual corruption despite their material wealth. He implored the people to return to the Lord and seek Him. He was a shepherd and keeper of sycamore trees until God called him to bear His burden.

The burden of the Lord to Prophet Obadiah was to preach to the Edomites. The

Edomites were the descendants of Esau. He preached God's hatred of the proud and their subsequent fall. God hated their arrogance and antagonistic ways toward Israel. His is the shortest book among the other prophets.

The burden of the Lord to Prophet Jonah was to preach to Nineveh. He was an evangelical prophet sent to preach salvation to a city about to fall under the judgment of God. His ministry also proved that God extended salvation to the Gentiles beyond the Jews. This did not sit well with Jonah; in this regard, he and Apostle Peter had a lot in common. His ministry proved that God is no respecter of persons. He loves all mankind and gives them all an opportunity to receive salvation.

The burden of the Lord to Prophet Micah was to pronounce judgment upon Israel and Judah and the doom that was heading their way. He then tells them that God will comfort them afterward and even restore the glory in

Zion. He preached deliverance from Babylon and prophesied the Deliverer from Bethlehem. He reminds them of what it means to worship the Lord purely and even reminds them of their deliverance from Egypt. Micah, a poor farmer, champions against the poor being unfairly treated by the rich.

The burden of the Lord to Prophet Nahum was to declare that God's justice and sovereignty would triumph. He prophesied Nineveh's destruction and God's retribution. He preached the vengeance of the Lord. Nahum taught the people that whoever resists the Lord will feel His wrath, and those who trust Him will be preserved.

The burden of the Lord to Prophet Habakkuk was to awaken the people to their need for the Lord. The prophet was disturbed by the increased wickedness in Judah, and he interceded for God to judge the people for their blatant sins. The Lord assured the prophet that

He would avenge Himself before his eyes.

The burden of the Lord to Prophet Zephaniah was to strike a reverent fear in the hearts of the inhabitants of Judah. He preached their need for repentance and promised mercy to those who returned to the Lord.

The burden of the Lord to Prophet Haggai was to call the people to rebuild after they had been delivered from exile. He rebuked the people for labeling God's work as secondary and only contingent upon improved economic conditions. He promised them that God would send help and give them a favor if they returned to work.

The burden of the Lord to Prophet Zechariah was to co-sign what Haggai said. God wanted His temple rebuilt, and the people were moving too slowly, so He sent reinforcement in the person of Zechariah. He was a prophet of confirmation who used many references to earlier prophets in His writings. His burden was to see the Kingdom of God fully established.

The burden of the Lord to Prophet Malachi was to deal with corrupt priests. Malachi pronounced a curse upon the unfaithful priests and those robbing God. He also preached against unbalanced marriages with unbelievers. He ended his ministry with a promise that the people of God would be restored in their relationship with the Lord.

Many other prophets in the Old Testament did great works for the Lord and carried His burden, but these prophets had an extensive ministry for the Lord. It is also noteworthy that major and minor prophets are man-made titles. God's prophets are important to Him, and no one except John the Baptist is greater than the other. Jesus said John was the greatest prophet who ever lived. And although many fail to acknowledge him, John the Baptist was the last of the Old Testament prophets, not Malachi.

-5-

New Testament/Covenant
Prophetic Ministry

1 Corinthians 14:39, "Wherefore, brethren, covet to prophesy, and forbid not to speak with tongues."

When the promise of the Holy Spirit was evidenced on the day of Pentecost as prophesied by Joel, every Spirit-filled believer received the ability to prophesy.

Acts 2:17, "And it shall come to pass in the last days, saith God, I will pour out of my Spirit upon all flesh: and your sons and your daughters shall prophesy, and your young men shall see visions, and your old men shall dream dreams."

Joel was prophesying to the ancients of Israel that their descendants would carry the 'now breathed' word of the Lord sometime in the future. Even the Lord Jesus, the Chief and Master Prophet, prophesied the following:

Matthew 4:4, "But he answered and said, It is written, Man shall not live by bread alone, but by every word that proceedeth out of the mouth of God."

Pay closer attention to what Jesus said. He said the time would come when a man would live by the logos and the rhema. To be successful and relevant in this season and hour, we need the written word and the spoken 'proceeding' word of God. We need prophetic people who are spiritual fountains of the Lord bubbling up our God's will, word, and mind.

The confusion among too many in the Body of Christ is the prophetic people falsely assume that they are prophets because they prophesy. This is a grave mistake and tragedy because a prophet's grace differs tremendously from a prophetic believer's grace. The difference would be in revelation, among many other factors. As we have studied from the Old Testament, prophets are mature, sound, precise, seasoned, obedient, and knowledgeable. And it's not that others aren't; it's just that they have supernatural insight beyond a *thus sayeth*. They possess an intellect out of this world with which they need to work alongside the apostles of Jesus Christ to build churches. They are not just *prophesiers*; they are builders. To build the church (human temples), the prophets teach, impart, train, rebuke, correct, raise, and tear down. The ability to prophesy what the Lord is saying and work alongside apostles to form the Church's government is profoundly different from that of a prophesier.

When we say build churches, we are not talking brick and mortar. We are discussing building, rebuilding, tearing down, and restructuring lives. You can recall the *burden to Jeremiah here in Jeremiah 1:10. "See, I have this day set thee over the nations and over the kingdoms, to root out, and to pull down, and to destroy, and to throw down, to build, and to plant."* Prophets require a tougher spiritual skin than a prophetic believer because their work is much heavier, more detailed, more dangerous, and very articulate. *Ezekiel 3:9, "As an adamant harder than flint have I made thy forehead: fear them not, neither be dismayed at their looks, though they be a rebellious house."*

While the prophetic believer may be called 'prophet or prophetess' by their gift, to stand in the government of the Kingdom of God is a heavy task that is not for the faint of heart. It is not for the double-minded, the sensitive, the carnal mind, the novice, the ignorant, the fearful, or the proud. The office of the prophet is a consecrated and holy office that is set apart. It is a different work designated for those who were called from birth.

Man does not appoint you as a prophet; they can't. They can recognize the *office* beyond the gift but cannot place you. They can paper you there by a certificate, but they cannot appoint you there. God called the prophet before the foundation of the world was framed, and He has seasoned and graced them with both spiritual gifts and abilities needed to accomplish the work for which they were sent.

Just because a prophetic believer is not a prophet does not mean God uses them any less. They will dream dreams and see visions. They will speak the word of the Lord. They will preach and teach. And they will even edify the believer, but they are not graced for the government in the Kingdom. Many have erred and have fallen away from the faith because they reached for a position presumptuously without the Lord's grace in that work. Even worse, God holds us accountable for what we say and do in His name, even when He has not licensed us to do so. That means that any work we lay our hands on that God has not authorized will be called to judgment, just like the work we were authorized and yet failed to accomplish.

Matthew 7:22, "Many will say to me in that day, Lord, Lord, have we not prophesied in thy name? and in thy name have cast out devils? and in thy name done many wonderful works?"

The prophetic people of the New Covenant/Testament are generally exhorters, encouragers, and edifiers. Their burden is to see people walking in a closer relationship with the Lord. They carry the burden of the Lord Jesus Christ to draw men to Him. They do this in worship, prayer, exaltation, and deed. Barnabas (birth named Joseph), a New

Testament prophet, was an encourager of the brotherhood. He was filled with the wisdom of God to teach people how to draw closer to the Lord. The people loved him so because of this ministry grace in his life that they nicknamed him the *son of consolation*. When the people needed a word of encouragement, they knew to turn to Prophet Barnabas.

Your gift will make room for you. Unlike in the Old Testament, when the prophets only came around in certain seasons, in the New Covenant, prophetic people are everywhere. They are not only in churches but also in the workplace, our communities, our families, and our friends. God has prophetic people everywhere because the harvest is now plentiful, but the laborers are few. The prophetic people feel the burden of the Lord, and they are strategically placed around each of us to consistently release the word of the Lord and confirm the word of the Lord that we continue to abide within the parameters of the destiny wherewith we are called.

Although there aren't nearly as many recorded New Testament prophets as there are in the Old Testament, they are mentioned and carry the burdens of the Lord. As I mentioned earlier, John the Baptist is the last Old Testament prophet, but he is recorded as preaching the message of repentance in the New Testament. Anna, the Prophetess, carried the burden of the Lord to bear witness on the earth and among the people that Jesus Christ was indeed the Messiah, the blessed Son of God. As the early church started, several prophets were ministering in the churches, and before Paul was called an apostle, he was recognized as a prophet.

Acts 13:1, "Now there were in the church that was at Antioch certain prophets and teachers; as Barnabas, and Simeon that was called Niger, and Lucius of Cyrene, and

Manaen, which had been brought up with Herod, the tetrarch, and Saul."

Considering that the early church was forming and surrounded by great persecution, the prophets were in high demand to teach the people and encourage them to continue doing the will of the Lord.

The more prevailing prophet in the New Testament, Agabus, was only mentioned twice in scripture. He was recorded for predicting a worldwide famine, and then he is recorded for his prophecy to Apostle Paul about his imprisonment in Jerusalem. Not much more is said of him, which shows that after Malachi, for about 400 years, the prophets went relatively unnoticed. It would take Apostle Paul to conduct entire teachings on prophetic ministry to train the next generation of prophetic people.

This page left intentionally blank.

-6-

The Lord's Burden For New Covenant Prophetic People

Romans 1:13, "Now I would not have you ignorant, brethren, that oftentimes I purposed to come unto you, (but was let hitherto,) that I might have some fruit among you also, even as among other Gentiles."

During the church age in which we are in, it is the will of the Lord to transition His people to a renewed mind in Christ Jesus. The Lord desires His people to walk after the Spirit and not fulfill the flesh's lusts. To do this, He sends prophetic people and teachers to instruct and guide them toward renewed thinking. The thoughts of a man are powerful enough to control the actions of a man; therefore, if the Lord can use prophetic people to grow and mature the minds of the believer, they can learn how to arrest ungodly thoughts and perhaps curve the physical responses to un-policed thoughts.

Proverbs 23:7, "For as he thinketh in his heart, so is he: Eat and drink, saith he to thee; but his heart is not with thee."

New Covenant prophetic people carry the burden of the Lord to prepare the hearts of the believer to manifest the Kingdom of God. Jesus preached that the Kingdom of God was near. Then He preached that the Kingdom of God was within the believer. The Kingdom of God is both spiritual and physical. There will be a physical expression of the Kingdom of God, but now there is a spiritual expression of the Kingdom of God that takes place in the believer's life.

Luke 9:27, "But I tell you truly, there are some standing here who shall not taste death till they see the kingdom of God."

Luke 17:20-21, "Now when He was asked by the Pharisees when the kingdom of God would come, He answered them and said, "The kingdom of God does not come with observation; nor will they say, 'See here!' or 'See there!' For indeed, the kingdom of God is within you."

Luke 21:31, "When you see these things happening, know that the kingdom of God is near."

Clearly, as in the mission and ministry of the Lord Jesus, New Covenant prophetic people will share the burden of the Lord in preparing the believer for the expression of the Kingdom of God on earth. This continual process tears down the walls and gates of religion to replace them with biblical truths, practical Godly living, and soundness in the faith. A kingdom is as strong as the people representing it. Therefore, God gave us all talents and gifts to help build His Kingdom. Jesus ascended and left spiritual gifts in the churches, and contrary to popular opinion, those gifts are not only spiritual but also physical. Those physical gifts are represented by humans such as apostles, prophets, evangelists, pastors, and teachers to train and mature the saints. Jesus calls forth His laborers, imparts them, and sends them out to bring in the harvest of believers unto the Lord. This labor-intensive work comes with tremendous demonic resistance, hence the need for spiritual maturity and soundness in the faith.

Satan saw what Jesus did with just twelve men, and he fought Him vehemently. What do you think about the warfare we will face as we reach and teach co-workers, family, friends, and nations for Christ? Apostle Paul was beaten, shipwrecked, imprisoned, and suffered tremendously for his labor in the Kingdom of God. You and I are no different; therefore, we are instructed to put on the battle gear.

Ephesians 6:11-18, "Put on the whole armour of God, that ye may be able to stand against the wiles of the devil. For we wrestle not against flesh and blood, but against principalities, against powers, against the rulers of the darkness of this world, against spiritual wickedness in high places. Wherefore take unto you the whole armour of God, that ye may be able to withstand in the evil day, and having done all, to stand. Stand therefore, having your loins girt about with truth, and having on the breastplate of righteousness; And your feet shod with the preparation of the gospel of peace; Above all, taking the shield of faith, wherewith ye shall be able to quench all the fiery darts of the wicked. And take the helmet of salvation, and the sword of the Spirit, which is the word of God: Praying always with all prayer and supplication in the Spirit and watching thereunto with all perseverance and supplication for all saints."

Apostle Paul suited us for the battle with everything we needed to succeed. Another critical point is that most of the Old Testament scripture is written by prophets, while the majority of New Testament scripture is written by apostles. Do you see the pattern? The apostles and prophets lay foundations, with Jesus Christ being the chief cornerstone.

-7-

The Burden of New Testament Prophets

Ephesians 2:19-22, "Now, therefore, you are no longer strangers and foreigners, but fellow citizens with the saints and members of the household of God, having been built upon the foundation of the apostles and prophets, Jesus Christ Himself being the chief cornerstone, in whom the whole building, being fitted together, grows into a holy temple in the Lord, in whom you also are being built together for a dwelling place of God in the Spirit."

New Testament prophets declare the Lord's message to impact others' lives. They receive supernatural visitations from the Father. They hear and see into spiritual realms. They carry the revelation of the Lord to instruct, govern, raise, tear down, confront, rebuke, set in order, remove, declare spiritual warfare, ordain, consecrate, and delegate. They have unusual abilities, greater strength, and fortitude, are creatures of habit, study God's word for hours on end, and can flawlessly articulate the Lord's will. Like their Old Testament counterparts, they know the heart of the Lord. They become one with His mind and understand His methods and emotions. *Unlike* their Old Testament counterparts, they are team players. They work closely with apostles and have the respect and submission of the evangelists, pastors, and teachers that God gave them through the protocol of ministry established by Apostle Paul.

Prophets are generous in their teachings, travel, and sit for hours expounding upon the word. They are worthy of being provided for by the Houses of God, as are the apostles. They can engage in profitable enterprises for themselves if they feel resistance in the form of monetary compensation or if they choose to refuse an offering. It is important to note that false prophets have corrupted the hearts of many against honoring the prophets, but God has not changed His word about it nonetheless. Even Jesus said that prophets would not be honored at home but would receive honor abroad. It is also important to note that every prophet who received honor returned a blessing in its place. That is the value the Kingdom of God has placed upon the prophet because of the tremendous sacrifices they have made for others in terms of their labor in the work of ministry.

Consider Saul giving Samuel an offering of silver and ultimately becoming king.

Consider the widow feeding Elijah, and Samuel raised him from the dead when her son died. Consider the Shunammite woman who made a particular room in her home for Elisha, took care of him whenever he came to town, and raised him back to life when her son died. Consider Barak honoring Deborah and winning the victory in battle. Consider Hezekiah honoring Isaiah, and when he was dying, God added fifteen years to his life.

In the New Testament, consider Jesus, who was always provided for in the house of Lazarus with his sisters, Mary and Marth. When Lazarus died, Jesus raised him back to life. Consider Mary of Magdala, who broke her alabaster box of expensive perfume to worship and anoint Jesus' feet. Consequently, she was the first to witness Jesus' resurrection. (She is also the first female evangelist.) I could go on, but do you understand God's honor on His prophets? He backs up their words, co-signs their instructions, and pours out signs and wonders as the fruit of their consecrated lifestyle.

The New Testament prophet carries the burdens of the Lord to see His people delivered, set free, walking in victory in every facet of their lives, and bringing souls into the Harvest of the Lord. They do this by teaching, discerning, envisioning, encouraging, inspiring, leading, commanding, prophesying, interpreting, and building people's lives. They are motivated by one thing and one thing only, LOVE. The sign of a New Testament prophet is that they are created to love God first and the people they serve. Prophets must carry an intense love life to carry the burden of the Lord because Jesus' placement in the earth was motivated by God's love. Again, the prophet of God must be motivated by love, not MONEY. Now, love does not mean agreeing with everything. Love corrects, instructs, and rebukes, but love draws men to the feet of Jesus.

Jeremiah 31:3, "Yea, I have loved thee with an everlasting love: therefore with lovingkindness have I drawn thee."

An entire discourse is written by Apostle Paul on the importance of love for prophets. Many fail to realize that although 1 Corinthians 13 is for everyone, it is specially written for prophetic people, for Apostle Paul was addressing believers with spiritual gifts.

1 Corinthians 13:1-13, "Though I speak with the tongues of men and of angels, and have not charity, I am become as sounding brass, or a tinkling cymbal. And though I have the gift of prophecy, and understand all mysteries, and all knowledge; and though I have all faith, so that I could remove mountains, and have not charity, I am nothing. And though I bestow all my goods to feed the poor, and though I give my body to be burned, and have not charity, it profiteth me nothing. Charity suffereth long, and is kind;

charity envieth not; charity vaunteth not itself, is not puffed up, doth not behave itself unseemly, seeketh not her own, is not easily provoked, thinketh no evil; rejoiceth not in iniquity, but rejoiceth in the truth; beareth all things, believeth all things, hopeth all things, endureth all things. Charity never faileth: but whether there be prophecies, they shall fail; whether there be tongues, they shall cease; whether there be knowledge, it shall vanish away. For we know in part, and we prophesy in part. But when that which is perfect is come, then that which is in part shall be done away. When I was a child, I spake as a child, I understood as a child, I thought as a child: but when I became a man, I put away childish things. For now we see through a glass, darkly; but then face to face: now I know in part; but then shall I know even as also I am known. And now abideth faith, hope, charity, these three; but the greatest of these is charity."

This page left intentionally blank.

-8-
The Burden of Service
as Prophets

Prophesy to the young, start with the young and build foundations and platforms of the word of God in their lives. Prophesy to the poor. Elijah released a word to a poor widow in Zarephath. She and her son were destitute, starving, and losing all source of hope in anything good ever happening for them. Elijah stepped on the scene, challenged her faith, and destroyed the stronghold of death. His prophetic ministry changed her life forever. Prophets bring change. We speak the word of God and don't focus on people's circumstances.

Prophets counsel from the heart of God. They walk in the supernatural, yet are not flaky, deep in revelation, and anointed. Prophets must watch what they say because what is spoken manifests; a shift happens. Prophets don't speak careless words. We speak resurrection and life.

Prophecy destroys the strongholds of the mind. It challenges your belief systems and pulls down faulty belief systems. Thus, prophets are to walk in God-conscience, not self-conscience. We are the sons (non-gender) of the most High God, called to occupy, take dominion and walk in authority. We walk in power, knowing God was intentional when He called us into this third-day dimension. We are a risen people; we rose with Christ.

Don't conform yourself to others, or you

will waste your oil. Remain true to who you are because the presence of an authentic prophet changes atmospheres. When you arrive on the scene, change occurs. Walk in the supernatural realm; expect the supernatural to respond. Walk with integrity before the Lord and His people. Watch your testimony.

Prophets have joy. This joy forms the basis of your strength. Prophets need strength to impart strength to those they serve. You cannot release that which you do not have. Consider how our bones need muscles because muscles provide strength, stamina, and structure. Be like that muscle that strengthens bones, the structure of a person's life. Be essential and substantial. As muscles provide shape to bones, you give shape to issues in others' lives with your words. Faith is a muscle to move mountains while skin covers muscle and bone. It is a protective covering for your internal systems. Therefore, prophets shape and provide structure, stamina, and cover. Prophets aren't intimidated by valleys of dry bones. You will know instinctively what needs to be said and done to restore life to those you serve.

Prophets walk in glory realms. You become another man. God abandoned the fruit of the tree of knowledge of good and evil. He would instead we eat from the fruit of the Tree of Life. It's not enough to know God; can you perform in God? You must eat Jesus' flesh and drink His blood - maintain constant communion with the Father. What you eat, you become. As you constantly feed on the Word, Christ, you become another man.

Declare over your life who God says you are, for He will bring you into your designated land, your metron. Know also that when God decrees over you, He speaks as a Husband. He plants and expects fruit. You must tap into that same 'husband' nature. Your words are seeds.

You are a seed carrier destined to plant rich words in the lives of God's people. Sow your seed generously, for God loves a cheerful giver (sower).

You will be assigned places of authority over which you are expected to take dominion. You must manifest a warring and firing spirit against wicked principalities at times. At other times, you must manifest a gentle spirit to restore the children's hearts to the Father. Know when you are to manifest the lion's anointing versus the lamb's anointing, for you carry this dual nature.

Do you recall the Prophetess Deborah in the Old Testament? She was also a judge and mother to Israel. Deborah functioned in several capacities but be mindful of her husband's position. Lamech's name means Light. The prophet must be married to the Lamech, the Husband of Light who exposes the darkness and provides illumination. No matter how many capacities in the prophetic ministry you possess, remain connected to the Light.

Consider who God called you to be. You will leap over walls, move in acceleration and perform great exploits. The devil can't latch on to you though; He will cause tremendous hindrances to slow you down. Nevertheless, God is establishing you, and you will not be moved from the place He has established for you.

As God is, so are we. You will walk in all God has released for you. His Kingdom has come in us; therefore, we legislate and enforce His Kingdom in this present realm.

Prophets operate in signs and wonders and should experience miracles every day. I see God's hand in my life every day. Also, be mindful of how you approach a matter. What you see is married to what you say. Don't be deceived by circumstances. You are a miracle worker, so perception does not always dictate reality. Perception determines reception. You should know that what people see and think about you does matter and what you see and think about them and their circumstances.

In terms of the dry bones I mentioned earlier, the way you approach the valley and the attitude that you bring will determine the bones' response to you. *Proverbs 13:17, "A wicked messenger falleth into mischief: but a faithful ambassador is health."* You can bring health and healing to people's lives, so take great care in how you approach their matters.

As prophets, we represent God in all we do. When our attitude is haughty, the people will feel as if the Lord is disgusted with them. I can't begin to share how many bitter and angry prophets I have met who instill fear by portraying the Lord as an angry, murdering God. Yes, there is a punitive side of God but also a restorative side. He is perfectly balanced, and we have to represent Him in truth. And just as you would despise it if someone misrepresented you, or falsified your identity, so does the Father when His character is mishandled.

For prophets, it's not just what you say but how you say it. The people who are submitted to your prophetic voice will learn about God's feelings through your mouth. And if you are fussing and ranting all the time, your people will develop into a nation of believers who think their God is angry with them. Couple this with the fact that many believers have problems with authority, particularly those who hail from loveless homes. You will trigger them and will have inadvertently distorted the image of a loving Father to a person who has never known true love. You will have done them a great disservice.

The balance is knowing when to be firm and direct and when to appear more compassionate. Learn the differences between the lamb's anointing and the lion's anointing.

This page left intentionally blank.

-9-

The Breath of the Prophet

In the previous chapter, I talked about the valley of dry bones. Let's spend some more time on this topic.

Ezekiel 37:1-14, "The hand of the Lord was upon me, and carried me out in the spirit of the Lord, and set me down in the midst of the valley which was full of bones, And caused me to pass by them round about: and, behold, there were very many in the open valley; and, lo, they were very dry. And he said unto me, Son of man, can these bones live? And I answered, O Lord God, thou knowest. Again he said unto me, Prophesy upon these bones, and say unto them,

O ye dry bones, hear the word of the Lord. Thus saith the Lord God unto these bones; Behold, I will cause breath to enter into you, and ye shall live: And I will lay sinews upon you, and will bring up flesh upon you, and cover you with skin, and put breath in you, and ye shall live; and ye shall know that I am the Lord.

"So I prophesied as I was commanded: and as I prophesied, there was a noise, and behold a shaking, and the bones came together, bone to his bone. And when I beheld, lo, the sinews and the flesh came up upon them, and the skin covered them above: but there was no breath in them.

"Then said he unto me, Prophesy unto the wind, prophesy, son of man, and say to the wind, Thus saith the Lord God; Come from the four winds, O breath, and breathe upon these slain, that they may live.

"So I prophesied as he commanded me, and the breath came into them, and they lived,

and stood up upon their feet, an exceeding great army.

"Then he said unto me, Son of man, these bones are the whole house of Israel: behold, they say, Our bones are dried, and our hope is lost: we are cut off for our parts. Therefore prophesy and say unto them, Thus saith the Lord God; Behold, O my people, I will open your graves, and cause you to come up out of your graves, and bring you into the land of Israel. And ye shall know that I am the Lord, when I have opened your graves, O my people, and brought you up out of your graves, And shall put my spirit in you, and ye shall live, and I shall place you in your own land: then shall ye know that I the Lord have spoken it, and performed it, saith the Lord."

Prophets are vessels by which the Lord brings restoration, resurrection, and reunification. Ezekiel was God's set prophetic man for that hour. He was summoned away from a dinner in his home into a realm in the spirit where an assignment awaited him. Although Ezekiel's physical body remained at dinner, his spiritual body was transported by the Spirit of God to a valley of dry bones. Recall when I mentioned earlier that prophetic people are people of the supernatural. We hear in the supernatural, see in the supernatural, and feel in the supernatural.

Many prophets, myself included, can attest to being raptured from a carnal gathering into the heavenlies where a message or an assignment is awaiting them. It is not unusual for prophets to be whisked away by the Spirit and transported to other realms to confront situations occurring in greater dimensions than where they presently are. This is what was happening with Ezekiel. There was an assignment to a graveyard of fallen soldiers who needed the Breath of Life. They were dead and needed resurrection, which would only fall from the lips of the prophet.

Can God trust you like that? Can He transport you to high dimensions in the spirit realm to breathe over marriage, a ministry, a family, or a business? Can He use your lips and lungs to revive what has been slaughtered by circumstances? Have you cultivated the capacity to hold the breath of the Lord until He authorizes you to release it? Can the Lord trust your opinion about a matter? Will you be honest during those times when He knows you don't know the answer?

The Lord positioned Ezekiel over the valley and told Him to look at it. Before we speak as prophets, we must first look at the matter. In other words, what have you discerned is taking place, has taken place, and will take place without prophetic intervention? What can your prophetic mind bring to this particular valley? How can you serve the Lord as His lips and tongue in this matter? When the

Lord brings your attention to a matter, it's not for you to speculate; it's for you to conduct a spiritual evaluation, a need base analysis, and determine the best course of action.

Prophets are lifetime members of God's Chamber of Decisions. He said He wouldn't do a thing unless He discussed it with His prophets. Don't read me wrong; I am not insinuating at all that the Lord needs our opinions! Not hardly! What He wants to hear is His counsel through your mind. It's as if He wants a symphony of voices surrounding Him that sounds like His. Reverberate His voice.

Prophet, can these bones live? Can this marriage survive? Can this ministry live? Can this relationship heal? The Lord asked Ezekiel the question, "Can these bones live?" Notice Ezekiel's answer. He said, "I don't know, Lord, but I am sure you do." In other words, he was honest with his feelings and said, "I don't know!" As prophets, we must remain true to our feelings. There is no need to appear super spiritual and pretend that we know all the answers when we don't. Why do we need to appear like we've got it all? Pride. We don't and will never have it all because the Word of God declares that we shall know in part, and we will prophesy in part. For now, we look through realms of the spirit through a darkened glass. Still, when the Lord appears, the uncertainty will be done away with because He will reconcile all things to Himself and remove the veil from our eyes. *1 Corinthians 13:12, "For now we see through a glass, darkly; but then face to face: now I know in part; but then shall I know even as also I am known."*

There is no prophet under the sun who has all the answers to everything; if they told you that they do, they have lied. God will intentionally veil things from us to keep us humble. *Psalm 55:9, "For as the heavens are higher than the earth, so are my ways higher than your ways, and my thoughts than your thoughts."*

In the Garden of Eden, when God made all things available to us, we chose, through Eve, to develop our sense of knowledge. As such, we have been banished from eating that particular fruit of knowledge. We have been made to study to show ourselves approved unto God, who in turn visits us with the revelation that we may acquire knowledge of spiritual things. So, for Ezekiel to answer the Lord by saying he did not know, he admitted his inferiority in understanding spiritual matters and thus opened the door for the Lord to make the revelation needed to complete his assignment.

Prophet, there is nothing wrong with telling someone you don't know the answer or that the Lord has not spoken to you on a particular issue. Be honest with yourself, your God, and those you have been called to serve.

You don't know it all. Even Jesus admitted that He did not know the day or the hour. If He, being the express image of the Father, confessed to not knowing the time of a particular season of redemption for the people of God, who in the world do we think we are? Humble yourself before the mighty hand of God that He may exalt us in due season. Getting low before the Father is your ticket to promotion in the Kingdom of God.

Ezekiel 37:4-6, "Again he said unto me, Prophesy upon these bones, and say unto them, O ye dry bones, hear the word of the Lord. Thus saith the Lord God unto these bones; Behold, I will cause breath to enter into you, and ye shall live: And I will lay sinews upon you, and will bring up flesh upon you, and cover you with skin, and put breath in you, and ye shall live; and ye shall know that I am the Lord."

Once the Lord captivated the prophet's mind with the disastrous scene in the valley and drove him to develop compassion for the state of the people, He released the command to prophesy. Without ever turning to the pages of 1 Corinthians 13, where the Apostle Paul laid love as the foundation for prophetic ministry, we find here that the Lord only partners with those who have a sense of compassion for the work He is calling them. It's relatively simple, in my opinion, to determine when your prophetic services are needed. Do you have compassion for the situation at hand? Do you care? Does it touch your heart? Has the Lord burned or imprinted the matter in your spirit? A careful review of the gospels would reveal that every miracle the Lord Jesus performed, even the casting out of devils, was directly related to His compassion for the people. Do you know how you can tell if a prophet has genuinely been released by the Lord to deliver a message on a matter? Study their spirit to see if you can find the spirit of compassion. Where there is no compassion, there is no faithful prophetic ministry. Why? Because Jesus is the fullest and most glorious expression of God's love for us, and since He is the Master Prophet, all of us prophets and prophetic people have been mantled under His prophetic authority and seal. If we do not smell like Him, talk like Him, taste like Him, walk like Him, and love like Him, we have not been sent by Him. Did He not declare in His word that without His Spirit, we are none of His?

Why does the enemy war against you so much? Why do the people you sent to help always end up hurting you, intentionally or not? Why does it seem that when you prophesy a breakthrough for someone else, you experience a breakdown for yourself? Because the enemy wants to frustrate you into throwing in your prophetic robe, cursing your mantle, and denying your birthright. Because Satan can't take what God has given you, he has to steal it, and the remedy to getting it from you is to provoke you into forfeiture. Why do you think Joseph's brothers had to strip the coat off him? Because he would not give it up.

How were they able to strip it from him? When he ventured past the place where his father Jacob sent him and invaded enemy territory without permission. Remember when Jesus was tested in the wilderness for forty days, and the enemy tried him? Satan said throw yourself down because the angels will catch you. Satan knew he couldn't take Jesus' life, so he put circumstances in place to cause Jesus to give it up. Even three and a half years later, the Lord Jesus' life was questioned. He said, *"No man can take my life. I have to give it up freely because I have the authority to lay it down and pick it back up again." John 10:18* Needless to say, the enemy can't take anything from you unless you surrender it of your own volition. Therefore, dear prophet and prophetic people, your warfare has been so intense because you have what the enemy wants. You have the power in your tongue to build while he can only destroy. *John 10:10, "The thief cometh not, but for to steal, and to kill, and to destroy: I am come that they might have life, and that they might have it more abundantly."*

The prophet is instructed on exactly what to say as the Lord gives Him the utterance. Prophets need to hear precisely what the Lord is saying because He does not respond to strange sounds. The Lord is absolutely under no obligation to water any seed He has not planted. Regardless of how good that word sounded and how eloquently it may have been delivered, shelve it because it will not come to fruition if that word did not originate from the higher heavens. The Lord honors His word, so much so that He honors it above His name. He even said heaven and earth would pass away before His word passed. Again, He said that His word is forever settled in heaven. Do you know how many people have built ministries, marriages, businesses, and relationships around prophetic words without God? It would blow your prophetic mind to know how many prophecies people are pursuing while foolishly believing that God has Fathered them. I shudder to think.

Dry bones are bones that have been exposed. In other words, some of our situations have had the wrong type of exposure. They've been exposed to the wrong thing or the wrong somebody for far too long. Anything exposed to air for an extended period of time dries out or becomes dehydrated (lose water). The enemy wants to keep the people exposed to the nonsense that dries them out, spends their water, and leaves them lying in graves as white-washed bones. The grave could represent a person's attitude or doctrine; it's a haven for dried-out bones. The word for air, breath, and spirit are all the same in Hebrew, *Ruach*, but not all Ruach is spiritual Ruach.

God wants to speak to the dry bones, but because He cannot legally operate in the earth realm, He has to partner with a prophetic voice to accomplish this task. You will hear religious folk proclaim all types of clichés such as, *God is good all the time and all the time, God is good. And if you take one step, God will make two. Or God can do anything but fail.* And even worse, *If He did it before, He will do it again!* All of those sayings are cute and quaint; the only problem is that there is no power in them. The Lord honors His word, not Mother Lemonade's favorite cliché!

You are a prophet with an apparent reason and are expected to carry His God's burden because God needs your voice to legislate justice and execute judgment in the earth. If the prophets don't speak it, it won't get done. Had it not been for Moses' mouth, Israel would not have been delivered from Egypt. *Hosea 12:13, "By a prophet the Lord brought Israel out of Egypt and by a prophet was he preserved."* When the Lord wants to move in the earth, He calls and looks for His prophets. He saw the devastation in the valley long before He called for Ezekiel. He saw it before it happened and before Ezekiel was born. Likewise, the same applies to you and me, situations were unfolding in the spirit realm long before you and I were even thought of, but the Father made provisions to handle that matter. He had Delisa in mind, and He had you in mind, and together, we can conquer and conquer in the name of our Lord and risen Savior and bring great glory to our Heavenly Father.

As Ezekiel prophesied over that valley of old, dried, whitewashed bones, he suddenly heard a noise. There was rattling and shaking as the pieces located one another, seeking out their fitting place, and joined themselves together. The prophetic word brings unity, stature, and tallness. What a beautiful image to behold as the muscles came upon the flesh, and the flesh upon the bone, and the bone is covered with skin. Here is the part of the prophetic process that takes place every time we prophesy.

First, we hear the noise. I think it's safe to say that noise and sound are two different things. A sound is distinguished, but the noise has no structure. You don't know where it came from, how long it lasts and to what purpose it serves. Is this not what happens when we prophesy? It seems as if the situation that we are ministering to becomes worse!! I remember when I taught this in our first-year school of prophets, and the class was relieved when I mentioned that the noise comes before the movement. In other words, the noise, the confusion, the frustration, and the nonsense that occurs when you prophesy is the prophetic indicator that movement is about to take place.

The noise results from the enemy's flinching as he is being robbed of the pieces and fragments he has stolen from you. The noise is the pricking and the prodding of those fragments finding one another. If you like quantum theories, it's molecules and atoms rushing together from their perspective places in the universe to make up the whole picture of things. It's the spiritual rush that brings order from chaos. It's the noise your human mind has translated into confusion by looking at it from the natural eye. The noise of the many parts being compressed and made to behave on your behalf, but God's not through yet.

Now that the prophet has brought order to the chaos, it's time to live. It's time for God to breathe afresh and bring new life. Herein is prophetic strategy revealed. We have to know when prophetic ministry is twofold. In this case, there was chaos and confusion, and before the

Lord can pour wine in this situation, He must first make sure there is a capacity to contain it. The wisdom in prophecy is knowing what to say and when. Perhaps the whole conclusion of the matter has been revealed as you minister to someone, but the timing of the Word is just as important as the word itself. Can you imagine what would have happened if the prophet commanded breath in the valley while they were still whited bones? There would be skin, bones, muscles, and flesh trying to coexist apart from one another because they all would have could breathe or live. But because the Lord waited until they were united and conjoined before He breathed life, they had no choice but to rise as one, a mighty army, focused and integrated.

Another clue to God's order in prophetic ministry is if it doesn't bring unity to the work of God, it is not the word of God.

When there was evidence of a *body* in the

valley and not simply *bones* in the valley, the Lord moved to another level of functioning. As pastors and leaders, we can determine from this holy passage what the Lord wants to see in our churches before He promotes and invites us to other realms in the spirit. The Lord wants to see the *Body*, not the members *(bones),* separately functioning. Jesus wants the sinews upon His Body. He bore the shame of nakedness on the cross, so we don't have to. Prophecy covers the body with sinews. Prophecy draws members of the Body to work together. God wants to see the sum of all the parts working together to form an army of One. This was Jesus' high priestly prayer. *John 17:21-22, "That they all may be one; as thou, Father, art in me, and I in thee, that they also may be one in us: that the world may believe that thou hast sent me. And the glory which thou gavest me I have given them; that they may be one, even as we are one."*

The Lord is only interested in unity;

therefore, if a relationship is broken, the first thing the Lord wants to do is bring the pieces together. Before He sends anyone to the nations with a passport and a flashy website, the Lord wants unity. Let there be peace, Jehovah Shalom, and then we build upon its foundation with the prophetic word of the Lord to repair, recover, and rebuild.

As a prophet, our breath carries violence in the spirit. When we pray, things change. When we worship, things change. When we preach, things change, and when we prophesy, things happen. When we speak, windstorms erupt in the spirit. When we speak, we disturb the prince's powers and rulers of the air. We challenge wicked spirits in high seats of authority. We displace territorial spirits. We break soul ties and generational curses, destroy roots of witchcraft, and frame worlds because the breath of the prophet contains the ability to be proactive within itself.

We don't wait for things to happen; as causative prophets, we cause things to happen. As Ahab called Elijah, the prophets of God are troublemakers. We incite wars between evil and good and call down God's fiery judgment on every enemy of God. We don't just like what we do; as prophets, we live what we do. That's our apparent reason, and this is our burden.

-10-
The Prophetic Attitude

We want to demonstrate the love of God, but we must also display God's sobering and very frank and direct nature. When the issue at hand is very serious in nature and time or opportunity is of the essence, you must be firm and very direct. When Elijah departed the Brook of Cherith and happened to meet the widow in Zarephath, he knew her situation was a dire one. He knew this woman was on her last leg and was out of faith, food, and fortune. Elijah had to use a direct and firm approach to get her to move quickly and obediently. She didn't have time to ponder or pray; she had to make a decision and do it now.

There are many windows or openings in heaven. One of those windows, as the spirit of God revealed to me, was called the window of one opportunity. God is the God of second chances, and He is also the God of the One and Only Chance. Too many saints gamble with this. There are certain privileges you will only get one opportunity to take advantage of. After that, it dies. The window of one opportunity has an expiration date. Just like your local drive-thru, the restaurant may close at a certain hour; there is that particular hour in the spirit that if you don't act within the parameters of that appointed hour, the window closes indefinitely.

The widow of Zarephath had been given such a window. She had one chance to make a life-and-death decision that would ultimately change the course of her and her son's lives forever. Thank God she chose life.

Further in the story, something chilling happens that teaches on the power of our words. Even though Elijah was on the scene to break the plague of death by starvation, the widow carried the authority in her home. When she released death on her and her son, death appeared. Nevertheless, when death appeared in her home, she took advantage of the window of one opportunity and entered into a covenant with the prophet. Elijah confronted the spirit of death, causing it to flee. This was a miracle performed by the prophet based on the woman's faith, covenant, and obedience. Did you hear that? I said she placed a demand on the prophet based upon their covenant, and he was obligated to respond.

Do you want to know why millions of believers suffer death in their situations daily? They miscalculated the time. They assumed their window of opportunity would remain open, missed God's voice through His prophet, and had no stock or audience in Heaven to respond to their request for help. Thank God for Jesus, who made way for us to repent of our sins and receive forgiveness. Thank God for grace and mercy. But why should we have to resort to that when we could have gotten it right the first time?

When Elijah spoke to the widow, he realized that *how* he spoke to her was just as important as *what* he spoke to her. No one takes you seriously while playing, laughing, and joking. It breeds an opportunity for the sin of familiarity to reproach your ministry when people become common with you. They will not take you seriously when you're too playful. Granted, there is a time for all things. Indeed, there is a time to laugh and a time to weep, but as the sons of Issachar, we need to know what time it is and abide within the parameters of that season.

As prophets, we carry the oil of prosperity. We have the anointing from the Father to speak, and Heaven engages what we say. Heaven is interested in what we say and responds to what we say because our words resonate with what the Father is saying. The Holy Spirit responds when we speak because we sound like the Father. In that, the Kingdom of Heaven should recognize our voice. Just as a child knows their parent's voice, heaven, hell, and earth know the Father's voice and that of His ambassadors.

This page left intentionally blank.

-11-
The Prophet's Burden of Prayer

Luke 18:1, "And he spake a parable unto them to this end, that men ought always to pray, and not to faint." When a prophet prays or intercedes, high-ranking spiritual authority takes place. Remember Daniel? He was no ordinary prayer warrior. He shook realms, changed events in time, displaced principalities, and attracted master angels, with the only flaw being his natural body falling under the weight of such intense spiritual activity. When a prophet prays, he loses virtue, energy, and strength. I know a few prophets, including myself, whom the Lord had to instruct on several occasions to eat a specific diet. The spirit of God will cause your body to crave particular food types after specific episodes of prayer or prophetic ministry. Sometimes, I would crave salmon, broccoli, spinach, peanut butter, chocolate, grapefruit juice, pickles, hard-boiled eggs, or just plain water. It is such an established eating pattern that when my husband takes me out for dinner, he always knows what my menu choices are: grilled salmon, steamed broccoli, and rice pilaf. I had no idea that during those times, the Holy Spirit was teaching me through my cravings which vitamins and minerals my body needed to sustain myself during the intense spiritual conflict. See the following verses.

Matthew 3:4, "And the same John had his raiment of camel's hair, and a leathern girdle about his loins; and his meat was locusts and wild honey."

Numbers 6:3-4, "He shall separate

himself from wine and strong drink, and shall drink no vinegar of wine, or vinegar of strong drink, neither shall he drink any liquor of grapes, nor eat moist grapes, or dried. All the days of his separation shall he eat nothing that is made of the vine tree, from the kernels even to the husk."

Intense spiritual ministry is very taxing on the human body. This is why God ordained and sanctified a day (or season) of rest. *Genesis 2:2-3, "And on the seventh day God ended his work which he had made; and he rested on the seventh day from all his work which he had made. And God blessed the seventh day, and sanctified it: because that in it he had rested from all his work which God created and made."*

Our physical frames are not equipped to function in intensive levels of spiritual activity for extended periods of time without demanding rest. We are terrestrial beings licensed to operate in the third dimension; therefore, we must be invited to these levels with God being fully aware our contact with Him on that level is restricted. Moses had forty days, Jesus (the man) had forty days, Jonah had three days, etc. It is imperative to wait for an invitation to breach the high heavens or risk astral projection.

Revelation 4:1, "After this I looked, and, behold, a door was opened in heaven: and the first voice which I heard was as it were of a trumpet talking with me; which said, Come up hither, and I will shew thee things which must be hereafter."

Revelation 11:12, "And they heard a great voice from heaven saying unto them, Come up hither. And they ascended up to heaven in a cloud; and their enemies beheld them."

Revelation 3:21, "To him that overcometh will I grant to sit with me in my throne, even as I also overcame, and am set down with my Father in his throne."

2 Kings 2:1, "And it came to pass, when the LORD would take up Elijah into heaven by a whirlwind, that Elijah went with Elisha from Gilgal."

The human body cannot and will not withstand extended contact times in the spiritual realm. If Jesus needed time to heal and be restored, what about us? *Mark 1:13, "And he was there in the wilderness forty days, tempted of Satan; and was with the wild beasts; and the angels ministered unto him."* I have seen many preach revival after revival, service after service, and the very next thing you know, they have crossed a point of no return and landed somewhere in the middle of the demonic realm. Your body needs rest. Exercise benefits little, the Bible says. Take care of your bodies. When Holy Spirit says, "Enough, it's time to rest," obey. God has dealt to every man a measure of grace. Know your measure and abide within the framework of your grace. Stay in your lane.

When there is an engaging and intensive spiritual activity, demonic or Godly, the human body reacts. For example, suppose an anointed minister lays hand on you to pray. In that case, the swift transfer of anointing may cause your body to temporarily suspend itself, causing you to fall backward, lose balance, or *be slain,* as the term is often used in charismatic circles. When you come in contact with that type of spiritual energy from the Heavenly realm, your natural body shuts down. It's like a tripped outlet plug that automatically powers itself down when the socket has been overloaded. Those moments of 'suspension' varies for each individual and are also based upon the measure of anointing and grace that the minister carries. Some people are 'slain' for a few moments, some for hours. This is a very real and tangible expression of the tangible power of God contained in the supernatural realm. The power transfer may also cause a person to jump, shake, shiver, and some may run. I overheard one preacher say that as the altar workers were praying with a particular individual, they jumped up and ran out of the church and down the street. Concerned for the person's safety, the members ran after the person, found them, and brought them back to the service. I can only imagine what the people in the neighborhoods were thinking, but clearly, the supernatural realm will always baffle the human mind. It is a higher realm that goes far beyond our understanding and reasoning. The Lord said His ways are not ours, and His thoughts are not ours.

The opposite of what I described occurs when contact is made in the demonic realm. When you encounter one operating in the spirits of psychic manipulation and know how to attack your mind with words, your body will react to its power, too. You may pass out and feel sleepy or dizzy. Fatigue sets in, resulting in sluggishness and lethargy because the thief comes to steal. He is stealing your strength. Consider how your body reacts if you ever wanted to know the difference between someone praying for you or preying on you. The spirit of God will quicken you or make you feel alive; the enemy, on the other hand, will cause you to feel drained. Granted, operating in ministry is tiring but know the difference between losing virtue and your will.

As prophets, you must know this. Many stand in line to receive a word from a person telling them they are a prophet, and the next thing they do is run off trying to pursue prophetic ministry. It takes time to pursue the prophetic ministry because everything about you must die. God does not want to use you, but He wants to use you as you are filled with Him. He wants to hear His sound dripping from our lips as we prophesy, not our emotions and certainly not the vain figment of our dark imagination gone wild.

I was already five years into my salvation experience before I began to pursue and carry out my prophetic ministry actively. Nearly twenty-five years later, I am still learning something new about the prophetic. I have learned that if you don't crucify your flesh, God will make sure to do it for you. This is not an overnight event, but as with anything, the more time it has to marinate, soak, age, or saturate, the better seasoned it is. Any good cook knows that the best tasting and most tender meat is that which has been resting and marinating for extended periods of time. Don't rush your process.

A generation of prophets has been soaking and marinating in Kingdom principles pertaining to the prophetic. These archers will bring Heaven down to earth as the knowledge of the word of the Lord pours from them like honey. Their words will sit on you and saturate the leaves of your life like the morning dew. Those pronounced words won't leave your side until the SON absorbs them back to Himself as those decrees are established in your life. They will release sweetness in the spirit realm that draws the presence of God like never before. They will displace the old order and prophesy the 'hell' out of your life.

These battle ax prophets will emerge mantled with a spiritual vest soaking in deliverance oil. Like Jehu, they will contain within themselves the power and swiftness as a drome of grain-fed horses.

We have been prophesying that God is doing a new thing, and rightly He is, but it won't be anything like what we have thought. A new people are performing this new thing; these are the prophets currently hidden in the caves. They are the ones you'd least expect to be God's choice mouthpieces. They will release the word of the Lord in a symphony like a God- orchestra. These prophets are His brass and woodwind instruments carrying a different tune but harmonizing in the spirit to form one sound. They will be His trumpets, horns, clarinets, flutes, saxophones, tubas, baritones, and trombones coming together in one accord with Kingdom minds forming a magnanimous crescendo that vibrates throughout all the spheres: the atmosphere, stratosphere, hemisphere, and troposphere.

This page left intentionally blank.

-12-
The Burden of Prophetic Maturity

Elijah was a prophet, a true God-man. In saying *man*, this is in no way tact to eliminate women in prophetic roles because prophetic ministry is a fathering ministry working alongside the apostle. Elijah was called the father of the prophets. Those who studied under him were called the prophets' sons. Men have seeds, and only seeds can reproduce after their kind. Jesus became the seed of God, the Husbandman, sown into the earth, even the lower parts of the earth, and He ultimately yielded a harvest in each of us. God sent His Son; He sowed His Son in the earth that we who believe in Him may live an abundant or harvested life.

Prophetic ministry is a training type of ministry. Much instruction comes along with prophetic ministry because great and extended teaching times must be involved to turn the people's hearts back to the Father. With so many running around claiming to be prophets, ask yourself the question. Have they taught you to draw nearer to God? Can they teach you how to find God's heart?

Love is the foundation for any genuine and authentic prophetic ministry, according to 1 Corinthians 13. If you don't have a love for God's people, He has not sent you to represent Him. Thus, when we speak of prophets as fathers, we consider them as building blocks of God's family.

Fathers bring stability, order, and discipline. The Bible declares apostles and prophets as the foundation of the Houses of

God, with Jesus being the chief cornerstone. If you've ever noticed, a house is only as spacious as the foundation. One may build many levels to increase height, but the foundation solely determines the width span. Once the foundation of a thing has been laid, its dimensions are established. What does that tell you? The extent to which a father is willing to stretch or expand is directly correlated to the amount of influence a family has. In terms of fivefold ministry building families of God across the nations, those governed solely by the pastor, the teacher, or the evangelist are more likely to soar in height. Still, their horizontal growth or sphere of influence is stunted without a foundation of apostles and prophets. Although they may accomplish incredible feats in ministry, there will have remained more they could have done through a greater sphere of influence with the apostles and prophets.

Lois and Eunice understood the concept

as it pertained to Timothy. As pastors, they reared Timothy in the word but were limited in spiritual influence because his foundation was missing; when they met Paul, an apostolic father, they released Timothy for mentoring and training under a higher spiritual order. Paul expanded Timothy's capacity to advance the Kingdom by adopting him as his spiritual father. Before long, Timothy was functioning as an apostle. What Lois and Eunice provided Timothy was essential and very strategic to his call. Still, the foundation he needed to expand beyond what his mother and grandmother taught him was imparted through Paul. Paul gave Timothy the foundation upon which he could build a more extraordinary, more impactful ministry.

A clearer picture of the importance of apostolic or prophetic fathers is painted for us in Jesus' ministry. When He called the apostles, they were first known as disciples or students.

Jesus, as the carpenter, was teaching them how to use the tools of the Word to build the Kingdom. Jesus contained every tool necessary to build the church and advance the Kingdom with his carpenter's belt. Each tool He possessed was of the highest quality; therefore, whatever Christ builds will last throughout eternity. You and I, the hammers and screwdrivers of the Lord, are to secure, tighten, affix, and stabilize the work of the Lord Jesus Christ, the Master Carpenter. Our nails and screws are the Holy Scriptures. We make repairs when needed. We demolish structures of religion and tradition. We raze roofs of hypocrisy, falsehood, and craftiness. The emerging apostles and prophets are still contained within the Lord's Toolbox awaiting their assignment and awaiting their season. The Lord has them covered, protected from the elements, and locked away until the appointed times.

The disciples had some training in the Word, but another level of understanding was needed to equip them as apostles. Jesus had to extend the influence of these men beyond their reputations of being fishermen and tax collectors. He needed to expand their knowledge and capacity of the Word of the Lord. The disciples were called to shake nations with the Word of God, not fish lakes, rivers, and streams. There was a clarion call to a more extraordinary fishing lake where you and I would be teeming, where the Holy Spirit's net could capture us and reel us in for God's Glory.

As with any form of teaching, the time comes when our lessons climax into testing times. As Jesus walked and talked with His disciples, it became expedient that they do not advance further in their teachings until they could prove to Him beyond unreasonable doubt that they understood and comprehended their apparent reason for following Christ. Jesus asked the disciples if they had yet to discover who He was. After nearly three years of intense training, the Lord wanted to know who embraced what was happening. He does us the same way as prophets. He wants to know that we know who He is. We can't effectively prophesy, pray or preach without the revelation of Jesus.

The Bible gives us the primary layout for ministry. Genesis is the beginning of the pattern of ministry. This is where we learn who we are, our purpose, and what belongs to us. Revelation is our destined end. We are to know who Jesus is, His purpose, and what all belongs to Him. We all begin with *Genesis* and are destined to find *Revelation*, and this is where the Lord challenges the disciples. Do you know who I am? Did you find the Revelation?

Peter received the revelation of Jesus. The other disciples missed it miserably. This shows you that if one-twelfth of the apostles missed the revelation of Jesus and walked with Jesus in person, what do you think of the many today who claim they know the Lord but have no revelation of who He truly is? Sadly, many are like most of the disciples who didn't know.

Peter said, "You are the Christ." The first attribute Peter acknowledged was Jesus' anointing. The word Christ in Greek is *Christos* which means *the anointed one.* In other words, Christ was not Jesus' last name! Remember I said earlier that the Lord God will always protect His anointing. The fact that Jesus was the Christ means that He was untouchable. He tells Pilate, "No man has power over me except what I give him." He said again, "I have the power to lay my life down and the power to pick it up again." Jesus is the anointed of God, and since His anointing abides within us, we have the same untouchability that He does. MC Hammer, once rapper now notable preacher, prophesied it rather well when he composed a rap song entitled, *Can't Touch This*. It is so; we cannot be touched unless God allows it.

Jesus blessed Peter once He received the revelation. When Peter *understood* the meaning of Jesus' name, Jesus gave Peter the disclosure of his name. He called Peter *the Rock*, upon which His church would be built. Suffice it to say that the church is not built on Peter but on the Rock (stone or foundation) upon which the revelation of Jesus Christ has been laid. Jesus also gave Peter the keys to the Kingdom and the power to bind and loose. These are *apostolic keys* to building the Kingdom and *prophetic keys* to release heavenly activity and bind demonic activity. These keys can open and close, established or remove.

As prophetic fathers in the faith, regardless of the number of sons we may nurture, there will always be those among the feet of the father who will grasp the revelation of who that father truly is and those who won't.

Those who won't still fulfill their work, but those who do will make up the pillars or columns of the Kingdom. They will embrace what they have been taught and apply every principle learned.

Prophetic fathers know by the spirit who their Peters are. They discern among their pupils and sons who the risk takers are, those with radical faith, those who will protect them as Peter did in Gethsemane, and who will bring them great honor despite the many failures in life and ministry they may make. Peters is full of loyalty, faithfulness, and determination. They may stumble and fall, but their zeal will help them back up to go farther than they've ever been. They know how and when to return to their set place because of their honor for their prophetic fathers.

The time will come for all we mentor in the faith to test what they have been taught. The Lord will let you know who has been paying attention and has heart knowledge of the Word versus head knowledge. Peter opened his heart, spirit, and womb to receive impartation - the seed of revelation from the Lord Jesus. God gave increase to the seed by watering it with an even greater depth of knowledge.

Notice how this works. As prophetic fathers, we build on a knowledge base and expand the person's influence on the earth according to the will of God. And if there is no knowledge base, but the person is willing to learn, we use that to add beams from there.

Elijah, a prophetic father, carried heavy weight in the glory realm. When one walks as a prophetic father, there is an intense anointing married to the assignment. The father in the prophetic operates on a stronger, more mature level of supernatural activity. And as with Daniel, there is another class of angels married to that assignment, just as another class of demons assigned to monitor your movements.

The danger of operating in a spiritual realm without Heaven's permission will bring great misfortune, despair, and shame. The sons of Sceva found this out to their dismay. They tried to imitate the apostles by casting out devils using counterfeit authority. They brought upon themselves swift shame and embarrassment.

We live in a time where the ministry has become quite the competition. With the innovation of technology and the resulting plethora of social networks, ministries are more visible and accessible than ever before. More ministries are using YouTube, Facebook, Clubhouse, and other streaming connections for their spiritual development. While that may be a good thing (because the sad but honest truth is many churches aren't progressive and ignore the members who are, and because there is no meat in the House), social media becomes the next stop for present truths. Combine this with the fact that many ministers are not necessarily walking in the fruit of righteousness. There are some reasons, among many others, why some believers are running to and fro seeking knowledge. Didn't Daniel forewarn us of these things? *Daniel 12:4, "But thou, O Daniel, shut up the words, and seal the book, even to the time of the end: many shall run to and fro, and knowledge shall be increased."*

Prophetic fathers have heavy mandates to accomplish, one of which is to raise the next generation after their kind. We see this mandate demonstrated with Elisha through Elijah. When Elijah called Elisha, Elisha ran back home to bid his parents farewell but noticed that Elijah continued walking. Prophetic fathers are not son chasers. Once a prophet releases the work or assignment, the burden remains upon that *son* to perform the task. Prophetic fathers are there to guide, not to babysit.

When Elijah's season of life and ministry

ended, Elisha was already in place to succeed him as the next Prophetic Father. Therefore, prophetic ministers must understand the importance of mentoring and fatherhood. We must abandon thoughts such as, "I don't need anyone over me. God talks to me too." Or, "He is a man just like me." Even worst, "I report to God!" From Genesis to Revelation, the word of God makes adamantly clear the expectation for submission to authority. Submission to authority is not limited to spiritual authority but also relational and civil authority. Apostle Peter prophesied a time when men would be lovers of themselves, boastful, proud, disobedient to parents, heady, high-minded, etc. I believe these are those times, and woe unto us for dwelling among a people of unclean lips, a wicked and perverse generation.

-13-
The Burden of Pronouncing Curses

I alluded earlier to the weight of spiritual authority prophetic fathers carry. I bring your attention to a matter occurring in 2 Kings 2:23-25 involving Elisha and several young people. *"And he went up from thence unto Bethel: and as he was going up by the way, there came forth little children out of the city, and mocked him, and said unto him, Go up, thou bald head; go up, thou bald head. And he turned back, and looked on them, and cursed them in the name of the Lord. And there came forth two she bears out of the wood, and tare forty and two children of them."* This passage thunderously conveys the might contained in the mouth of prophetic fathers.

Elisha was headed to prayer. He was headed to Bethel, the House of Bread, a favorite place of prayer for the prophets. As he was en route, he was approached by several young people who verbally assaulted and humiliated him. If you are an amateur student of the word, you might think Elisha overreacted and that he shouldn't have taken the young people's rantings so seriously. After all, kids will be kids. A more diligent student of the word will reveal the culture of Elisha's time and why what these children did brought the wrath of an angry God upon them.

Elisha was very well known in Bethlehem. After Elijah's departure, Elisha became the prophetic father and the subsequent chancellor of all five schools of prophets. Everyone in the region knew who he was, and the authority God bestowed upon him from Elijah. Therefore, it was common knowledge to honor the prophets, especially the senior prophet, whenever he drew near because he carried the precious word of the Lord. In this case, because Israel entered into a state of complacency and spiritual decay, the people were at ease in Zion, and with such reverence and honor for prayer, the word of God, and especially respect for the prophets, became a thing of the past.

The young men laid eyes on Elisha, teased, and poked fun at him. They called him offensive names, specifically "Bald head." Again, one might think that Elisha was a bald man and that being called a baldhead was not necessarily an insult. Still, for the sake of this story, he may or may not have been bald, but to be called as such was a direct insult to his prophetic mantle. From a cultural point of view, the boys were cursing Elisha and mocking his ministry. To be bald in Elisha's day was considered a shame and a disgrace. And when you consider Elisha an older, much wiser gentleman, you may wonder why these children called the prophet a bald man.

Venturing further, pay attention to what else they were saying about Elisha. "Go up, go up!' They were mocking Elijah's chariot escort into glory! As young people, how would they have known anything about Elijah's ascent had it not been told to them by their parents? These young people were mocking Elisha and making light of God's chosen method to deliver His weary son, the prophet Elijah, home to glory.

Parenthetically speaking, when a nation, church, or family rejects God and loses passion for the things He loves, prayer flies out the window, and respect and honor for God's servants also take flight. What was so significant about what these young men said and did to the prophet was that they represented a generation who despised God.

They were the fruit of their parents' backslidings. And for them to harass the prophet, they were simply repeating what they overheard their parents say about the anointed of God. Elisha witnessed firsthand a generation of young people who did not know God, did not fear Him and refused to revere the ones He had sent. The mocking of Elisha by these young people was in direct reproach to the God of Israel.

Isn't that what is happening in our culture today? Do we not see the lack of reverence for the things of God in our modern society? Have we not become a society of people who assault the Lord's ministers with names (false, fake, weird, long-winded, funny looking, etc.)? Do we not mock that which is holy? How many videos of church services have mocked and ridiculed the things of God? Have we blasphemed Holy Spirit by misapplying the works of God to that of Satan? Now, do you see why the prophet had to use stern discipline in dealing with these young people? What Elisha had experienced was not just an insult to his mantle but an all-out attack against the very heart of God, his prophetic messengers. Shall we not react so direct when the enemy has dared to breathe an insult against the God we love and serve? Absolutely. *Psalm 105:15, "Saying, Touch not mine anointed, and do my prophets no harm."*

Our modern society has television shows, plays, movies, songs, books, website pages, and more depicting our nations and world's disregard for what our Father deems sacred. I won't even mention what many of our churches have become; that's another book! But when we see the total disregard and disrespect for our God, we will also see the Hand of God moving to defend His name. In many cases, He will use the prophets to release the word that allows Him to do so. Because God gave dominion in the earth to man, all spirits, His and the enemy's alike, operate illegally in the physical realm without our permission. This is why your prophetic voice is so vital. God needs you to partner with Him so that He can exact justice on the earth. Be mindful that we don't solely speak so that He brings justice to the earth. Our God is just; therefore, we should also want to see His righteousness go forth to the saving of souls as well.

The Lord despises those who murmur against Him. And He has no respect of persons in terms of who He will visit. When the children of Israel were delivered from Egypt and grew miserable in the wilderness, the Lord destroyed an entire generation based on their murmuring and complaining. So to avenge about forty-two children and their parents on behalf of His prophet was actually an act of mercy compared to how He has moved against His enemies in times past.

Those young people offended Elisha and his mentor, Elijah. They were repeating what their parents were saying behind Elisha's back; they were the whistleblowers. Though they thought they were offending Elisha, they were reporting on the consensus of the people about their feelings toward their God. They despised the prophets, and to their horror and shame, their children were bold and brazen enough to make light of it to Elisha's face.

Our churches are no different. Adult members attend service before they arrive home and while their children are buckled in the back seat, they are harping on what's wrong with the church. They run down the pastor because his sermon didn't make them run and shout. They run down the choir because they didn't sing their favorite song. They run down the sisters because of their dresses and the brothers because of their suits. They put their mouths on everything God holds dear and then wonder why their children despise attending church. They wonder why their children have no respect for the House of God. They wonder why our nation's children are in harm's way. Have we considered the why? These terrible things are not always the result of a parent's sins, but what has happened to cause our children to be targets for the enemy they have become? Why has everything that touches our children become toxic to them? Why are our children constantly in harm's way from food, education, and entertainment? Could it be that what is happening is a corporate result of neglect at the expense of parents who have taken their eyes off their God? Have our modern-day parenting approaches swung open the gate for the She bears?

Elisha was not without recourse; despite the jeers and taunting, he had to maintain a sense of duty as a prophet and reprimand those ill-behaved and ill-mannered children by speaking a curse upon them in the name of the Lord. Let's look at why Elisha was not acting like a witch in speaking a curse upon the children and why the curse did not causelessly come.

As a prophetic father, it was Elisha's duty to correct and discipline among instruct, train, teach, and guide. Without it, there would be no balance, and a false balance is an abomination. Prophets cannot always proclaim blessings and favor; at some point, the Lord will require them to confront the people's sins, sometimes very sternly, whether they want to or not. They are compelled to obey than to sacrifice in all matters. Therefore, even if Elisha wanted to cast off the young people's actions as frivolous childhood antics, he couldn't because when they attacked him as a prophet, they also attacked the office of the prophet and the God who sent him. These young people insulted Elisha's assignment and the God who commissioned it. The direct insult against Elisha was an indirect insult to the Lord, who didn't think it was fun to play childhood games. The Lord required Elisha to curse those children in His name. It was not Elisha's idea, so he was not acting out of damaged emotions. He was executing a sovereign command under direct orders to do as instructed.

It may be challenging for a person who loves children to understand what's about to take place between God, Elisha, and those young people. Still, looking at these matters from a spiritual standpoint, you must understand our Father's reasons for decreeing such swift judgment to fall. It is also necessary to add that our thoughts are not like God's. He sees far above what we could ever imagine. He knows what lies in the core of a person's heart. Our human intellect is a shadow of how our Father engages in what He does. Much of what He does will not make sense until He decides to open your mind to receive His revelation and understanding. Thus, without His mind, there is no way you will be able to comprehend His ways or His thoughts. *Romans 8:7, "Because the carnal mind is enmity against God: for it is not subject to the law of God, neither indeed can be."* In other words, the way we think and have been processed to think goes contrary to God's very nature.

Do you see why it takes time to prepare a prophet to handle the Word of the Lord? The Holy Spirit has to baptize and renew everything about you. You cannot hold on to your thoughts while delivering the Word of the Lord, or you will compromise His message. Worse, you may misrepresent His heart to the people He loves unconditionally. We tread dangerous grounds in cases like these; therefore, we must be very careful to set a guard over our hearts and a door to our lips.

Those young people who teased the

prophet may have been viewed as just children, but the Lord saw them as an emerging seed of people who would threaten and perhaps even hinder His redemptive work. Let's be clear. Anyone hindering you from interceding and praying for others become enemies of God because, as I stated earlier, prayer releases His Hand to move in the earth realm. Therefore, whosoever stands in a believer's way of executing an assignment becomes an offense to the Kingdom of God. Notwithstanding, those young people represented a generation of those who would show great disdain and disrespect for the people of God and the things the Lord holds dear to Himself, particularly prayer and His prophets. It was, therefore, incumbent upon the Lord to impress upon Elisha to strike those young people with a curse. The matter came before the Lord for judgment, and Heaven would not relegate it as childish antics. What the enemy moved those young people to say was more than taunting and teasing; they were slapping our Father in the face. As a result, He inspired Elisha to pronounce the curse, for He chose which judgment the curse would bring.

This brings us to another very important point regarding the burdens of prophetic people. When and if the Lord moves upon the prophets to pronounce a curse, we have no jurisdiction over the manifestation of the curse, the duration of the curse, or those affected by the curse unless the Lord reveals it. We must learn to say what He moves us to and leave the remainder of the matter to His discretion. This is a hard thing, but Elisha had no idea what the manifestation of the curse would be. Perhaps he may have warned the children if he did; instead, he rebuked the children and continued on his way to prayer. He didn't hang around to see if God would co-sign the curse. It wasn't his business, and neither did he make any attempt to make it so. Once he released the word, his assignment was completed, and persisting in prayer is what ruled his day, not waiting to see what would happen to his enemies. May we be thus minded. Once the Father instructs us to deal with a matter, consider it dealt with. Watching and peeping around corners to see what is happening in so and so's house or so and so's church are all signs of immaturity and faithlessness. Speak the word and continue on your assignment. The Lord will ensure that you receive a report of what takes place. Just as in Job's case, someone will find you and bring you a report. Discipline your spirit to trust God, for if you indeed hear from Him, you won't need to sit around waiting to see what will happen. Keep working, and the report will find you.

Once Elisha partnered with the Lord as His mouthpiece, the Lord could exact vengeance on His enemies. Again, you might say, these are just young people, but from the realm prophets must navigate in, these young people represented an upcoming generation of God-haters and prophet stoners. They were the fruit of their parents' backslidings, murmurings, and complaining. Their parents corrupted them, and they, in turn, would have produced a generation worse than themselves. They had to be stopped, all bystanders had to be strictly warned, and the parents had to be condemned for using their mouths to destroy the lives of their seed. God is not playing, and He takes no prisoners. *Matthew 12:30, "He that is not with me is against me; and he that gathereth not with me scattereth abroad."* There is no shade of grey.

The cursing of the rebellious young people by the prophetic father Elisha is a very sobering subject. It should wake up and shake sense into all of us. People need to understand how God feels about His anointed. We also must understand how He feels about Himself and get wise about it quickly. When the Lord says not to touch or offend His anointed, He is not just talking about the person. He is referring to the investment or deposit of Himself into a person to further His work in the earth. God responds to God; therefore, when His anointed are offended, He is offended. *Exodus 15:3, "The Lord is a man of war: the Lord is his name."*

If you are found in the boxing ring of life with God as an opponent, you are in deep waters of trouble. God is very serious about protecting those whom He sends to accomplish His will in the earth. He will use unorthodox methods to avenge them if He has to, but He will not leave them comfortless. Vengeance belongs to Him. The anointing must not be tampered with; the Father won't tolerate it under any circumstances. He will use floods, lightning, storms, and hail to war against such. He will enter man's dreams to warn them about His anointing. He will even call animals as a witness against such to protect His anointing.

The Lord is just in His ways but does not fight fairly!

As Elisha continued to Mt. Carmel (the place of fruitfulness and plenty), the scene where the young people were turned drastic and horrifying. After the Lord made sure Elisha was out of the way, He called his servants out of the wilderness to avenge Him of His adversaries. God had already warned Israel about walking contrary to Him. His word is true, and He cannot lie. *"And if ye walk contrary unto me. . . . I will also send wild beasts among you, which shall rob you of your children," Leviticus 26:21-22.* Surely enough, the Lord called for the wild beasts, the bears, which tore the flesh of forty-two young people. We should also mention that there were other young men present who the bears didn't touch, so we see God's Hand of mercy intervening even in His wrath. Those bears agreed with the Lord God Almighty that a wrong had been done, emerged from their place in the woods, and executed judgment. Justice was served.

The Lord used very severe tactics in dealing with the enemy. He made a strong and obvious point not to touch His anointed. He also sent a sobering message to all of Israel about Elisha as a prophetic father, the authority he carried, and the respect he deserved. Notice how Elisha also revealed his nature in how he conducted himself by demonstrating temperance and wisdom. He said only what the Spirit of God permitted him to say and released himself from the situation. He didn't stay to argue or debate with the children. He didn't call chariots of fire or shooting stars from the sky. He didn't misuse or abuse his authority. He didn't try to take God's place as Judge. He moved out of the way and gave space to the Lord to finish what needed to be done.

The burden of prophetic fathers is to trust God for everything, including provisions and successors. They know which spiritual gifts need to be activated and when. Once, enemy soldiers surrounded Elisha and his servant, and when the servant became afraid, Elisha prayed that God would open his eyes to see into the spiritual realm. Elisha knew when to perform miracles. He knew when to cause the borrowed ax head to float to the surface and what blend of herbs to put into the pot of death that the sons of the prophets lived. He understood the strategy of the Lord to end famine just as Elijah understood how to end the drought. They know who to anoint, when, and for what assignments. They know these things because they are prophetic fathers.

The office of the prophet comes with great responsibility, intense preparation, and a life devoted and sold out to the word, not the world. Nothing is more disgusting and upsetting than encountering a person impersonating a prophet by intruding into the office. The primary reason millions have been deceived by the false prophetic ministry is that there is no depth of the word in them to guard against and defend them against demons of deception, and that is also a burden of true prophets.

ABOUT THE AUTHOR

Apostle Dr. Delisa Rodgers Butler is the Senior Pastor of The Love Church Charlotte in Charlotte, NC. She earned her undergraduate in human service studies from Queens University of Charlotte. She also earned her doctorate in theology from Tripp Bible Institute. Delisa is gainfully employed in her local public school district as a Professional Development Coordinator and supports her community as Executive Director of her nonprofit, Barbara's Lighthouse Resource Center. Delisa is married with five children and resides in Charlotte, NC.